THE DESIGNS
OF
LÉON BAKST
FOR
THE SLEEPING PRINCESS

THE DESIGNS
OF
LÉON BAKST
FOR
THE SLEEPING PRINCESS

A Ballet in Five Acts after Perrault

Music by Tchaikovsky

Preface by André LEVINSON

LONDON : BENN BROTHERS LIMITED
8, BOUVERIE STREET, E. C.
1923

First published in 1923 in a limited edition of 1,000 copies.

This edition published in 2021 by

The Noverre Press

Southwold House

Isington Road

Binsted

Hampshire

GU34 4PH

ISBN 978-1-914311-29-1

© 2021 The Noverre Press

PORTRAIT OF LÉON BAKST

by PICASSO

THE SLEEPING PRINCESS

BEFORE attempting to measure the influence and importance of the production of *The Sleeping Princess* in London, on November 2, 1921, when Serge de Diaghilev and Léon Bakst revived the ballet in so wonderful a setting, one cannot but recall the memorable evening of January 3, 1890, at Saint-Petersburg, the evening of its original production.

Not even thirty years have availed to diminish the vogue of this work, which, though possibly not superlative in itself, is most truly representative of the heroic period of the Russian ballet, the period upon whose transmitted glory the old Imperial Theatres have thriven down to our own day. It is a period, too, to be remembered for the introduction of Russian music to the stage, for the renascence of scenery and setting, and for the almost total eclipse by Russian dancers of the great Italian virtuosi, who for half a century had remained without rivals.

The original version of *The Sleeping Princess*, at Saint-Petersburg, was due to the collaboration of Marius Petitpa, master of the ballet, Vsevolojskoi, the director of the Imperial Theatres, and Tchaikovsky, the composer of the score.

Let us, therefore, examine the personality of these three men, who in this fairy-ballet constructed, from one of Perrault's tales, a masterpiece of the Russian stage, and consider what part each one of them played in the collaboration. That, I am sure, will be the best means of doing homage to those who in our own time have undertaken the task of bringing to the European stage such splendid echoes of a departed glory.

The Petitpa Dynasty

It is the privilege of those who maintain themselves by a living tradition, by an uninterrupted continuity, to form artistic "dynasties" wherein the mysteries of their calling, those complex and imponderable elements which constitute what we term style, are transmitted from father to son. Thus it was with the illustrious dynasty of Danjuro, that dominated the stage at Tokio for over a century. In their case the name, curiously enough, was perpetuated and rendered increasingly famous by a process of selection whereby it was transmitted not necessarily from father to son but to the best pupil. In the same way we see celebrated dynasties—cemented, however, by family ties—governing the art of the ballet. That of the Vestris supplied three generations of dancers. The Taglionis, who included in their ranks two ballet masters and three ballerinas, held despotic sway in Berlin, after having first conquered Paris. And finally, the Petitpas, a family of Marseilles dancers, were called upon to steer the destinies of Russian stage dancing.

Jean-Antoine, the father, a friend of Talma, taught at the Imperial School of Dancing at St. Petersburg, and joined his son, Marius, on the boards of the Grand Théatre Marie. Later, Marie, his beautiful grand-daughter, was first character dancer on the same stage in succession to her mother, *née* Surovchtchikova. Marius Mariusovitch, the grandson, abandoned the ballet for Russian comedy (in which he distinguished himself and was followed by two great-grandsons), while Liuba and Nadedja Petitpa remained true to dancing. That, in all, represents over a century of the stage. But, in addition to this, the annals of the Paris Opera include the name of Lucien Petitpa, elder brother of Marius, the protagonist of Gisella and Carlotta Grisi's dancing partner, who was described as "a clever mime" by Gautier, *"gracieux, passionné et touchant."*

But it was Marius who was destined to establish the Russian ballet in all its incomparable splendour. He remained in command under four Czars and eight directors, for nearly sixty years, the "ethereal" Perrot's successor. He staged fifty-seven new ballets, reconstituted seventeen and, in addition to this, composed the ballets for thirty-four operas. He, who had played the part of Phoebus with Elssler-Esmeralda, gave Mlle. Anna Pavlova her first part as "prima-ballerina."

Before he arrived in Saint-Petersburg, in 1847, his life was not rich in adventures. Born in 1822, he first appeared on the stage at the age of eight, when he played the part of a little Savoyard coming out of a magic lantern at the Théatre de la Monnaie, at Brussels. An obedient son, he overcame his initial dislike for his father's profession as well as his then apparent lack of vocation for it, and began his career at the age of sixteen, at Nantes, as first dancer and ballet master. Following a journey to the United States, which turned out disastrously owing to the impresario's lack of good faith, he went to Bordeaux, where he staged many ballets, and from there on to Madrid. Here began a brilliant episode in his career—an enthusiastic public, serenades, masks, cartels, pistol shots, a tour through Andalusia, the fandango danced in the midst of a delirious crowd at the fair of San-Lucar. The memory of these splendours remained ever fresh in Petitpa's mind, and during the rest of his life he was able to draw freely from them when composing innumerable Spanish dances, such as Glazunov's *Pandora*, the "fandango" in *Carmen*, or Minkus' *Don Quixote*, an entirely Spanish ballet. After a brief appearance at the Paris Opera, where he danced a *pas de quatre* with the Elssler sisters and his brother, he was summoned to Russia by a letter from the old master, Titus, and arrived on the Gagarine Quay at Saint-Petersburg in May, 1847. His first production there was *Paquita*, after Mazilier, with music by Deldevez. It has remained popular ever since, and its final *grand pas* constitutes one of his shining glories.

Petitpa's arrival in Russia coincided with the great romantic revival of dancing. The classical style of dancing, amplified, exalted and vitalised by the fever of 1830, had become stabilised, and popular dances (either authentic or adapted), from Spain and Germany, incorporated. In a word, the transformed ballet provided him with every opportunity for developing his talents, and he made use of this fact in masterly fashion. One can say that he created the Russian repertory almost in its entirety, sometimes, it is true, seconded by the obscure but exquisite talent of Leon Ivanov. He was never replaced, and with him disappeared the great traditions which he represented. It was by reacting against this tradition that Michel Fokine imposed himself; amongst those true to the classical ballet, none was strong enough to resist so vigorous a thrust.

For some twenty years Petitpa maintained his position alongside of Perrot and Arthur Saint-Léon, the famous dancer-violinist; from

1870 onwards his power was absolute. The ballet, *The Daughter of Pharaoh*, taken with the assistance of Saint-Georges from Theophile Gautier's *Romance of a Mummy* and inspired also by the Egyptian collections of the Berlin Museum, assured his triumph. Since 1862 it has never left the programme, and exists unaltered, together with *The Bayadere*, which is fifteen years younger. The period of Vsevolojskoi's directorship brought a whole series of masterpieces. Petitpa created *The Sleeping Princess, The Lake of the Swans* (which had been a failure eighteen years earlier at Moscow), and *The Nutcracker* with Tchaikovsky; and *Raymonde, The Four Seasons* and *The Trial of Damis* (an act in the style of Watteau) with Glazunov. In this manner Russian music at last penetrated a new domain. These principal works, together with *Harlequin's Millions*, by Drigo; *The Butterfly's Caprices* and *Gisella*, revised after Coraly; *The Corsair*, after Mazilier; *The Hunch-Backed Horse*, a popular Russian ballet, after Saint-Léon; *Esmeralda*, after Perrot; *The Badly Guarded Daughter*, an adaptation of the ballet by Dauberval and, therefore, in respect of both design and traditional stage play, dating back to 1762; and, finally, *Coppelia*, by Delibes; form the imperishable foundation of the Russian choregraphic stage. With increasing frequency new works, having as a rule first proved their worth at Paris under Diaghilev, are added to this "Petitpa foundation," but without losing any of that impressive unity and coherence which is the result of a unique and bewitching conception, the cult of classical dancing. To-day, as in the past, nobody can even become a "super" in Russia without first being broken in by the discipline of "exercises" for eight years, and nobody can become ballerina before having triumphed in one of those romantic, if somewhat disconnected works, with decayed scenery, tattered costumes and music reminiscent of the barrel-organ or a travelling circus.

That is how these ballets, which are truly ageless, come to command only the purest genius of dancing.

Characteristics of the Classical Ballet

A minute examination of the style of Petitpa would carry me far beyond the limits of this preface, so that a summary sketch must suffice. The "ancient ballet" consists essentially of a series of dances bound together and co-ordinated by dramatic action. This dramatic action is expressed by means of pantomime with conventional gestures, and it is joined to the music only by the dynamic links of the emotion expressed. But this inherent dualism of pure pantomime and abstract movements of dancing is modified by a process, the *pas d'action* wherein every movement of the dance is dictated by the dramatic situation and linked to it by the actions, mimicry or gesticulations that interpret the feelings of the actors. The dance itself is amplified: the so-called character-dance reverts to the true fountain-head, its popular source, the local motif being adapted within the boundaries provided by a "classical" education.

The classical dance can be succinctly characterised by the use of beats on the points and beats of *élévation*. It contains the traditional, symmetrical forms of the *pas de deux*, a choreographical poem in three verses in a rigid frame-work:—the adagio, which is a chain of movements and pirouettes by the ballerina supported by the dancer; the two variations, that of the ballerina and that of the dancer, whose more restricted art is confined to leaps, the entrechat and series of pirouettes; lastly the *coda*, in which the dancer alternates with the ballerina in a succession of accelerated measures that mount up to the presto and end in a whirlwind of movements and dizzy complicated turns, crossing the stage diagonally.

At other times the diverse and complicated dance of the ballerina is accompanied by uniform and powerful movements of the whole *corps de ballet*. In Russia the latter is by no means reduced to playing the subordinate and purely decorative part of a mute chorus. In the *ballabili* it goes through its evolutions to the rhythm of a waltz or march, a complex organism moved by a single will. *Soli* detach themselves from this living orchestra, standing out vigorously against the compact background and then sinking back into the ensemble.

In Europe, in Paris, the arrival on the scene of the great virtuosi was the origin of the decline of the *corps de ballet*, which was relegated by their appearance to a purely decorative position. In Russia, on the other hand, it was this section which for a long while gave the ballet its true national character and was its principal source of supply for fresh talent. Rejuvenated annually by reinforcements coming from the school and by the departure of members having accomplished twenty years of service, it was the final factor (it is not long since it excited Gautier's admiration) that assured their supremacy to the Russian ballets.

The subjects of all these works and their settings were taken from more or less precise historical and geographical sources, such as India, Spain, mediæval Germany, the Directoire and the Rococo period, Lydia of the time of King Candaules or Hungary at the time of the Crusades. The costumes and types in the character dances were adapted from these sources; the scenery was based on the archeological conceptions of the last century. The classical dance alone, with its ideal essence, its system of formulæ and symbols, independent of sentiment and aloof from realism, constituted a common unchanging element throughout, governed by constant laws. Thus the traditional *tutu* paraded its immaculate whiteness against the backgrounds of Hindu festivals of Egyptian fantasies. At the most, some small national emblem, a cockade, a cap or a veil, linked the peasant of the Hungarian puszta or the Bengali bayadere to their native soil. Such, briefly expounded, were the general characteristics of the Russian classical ballet, the ballet of Petitpa. Who could assess in its entirety the "estate" this genius left behind him, the capital he made out of the classic style? He was an inexhaustible inventor of movements and groupings, with a faculty for co-ordinating masses on both a grand and a miniature scale. I have seen on the unpublished manuscripts of his programmes tracings determining the exact point for every dancer to stand when at repose, forming a complete picture. To such a point did Petitpa occupy himself with the plastic whole, with harmonizing the "dynamic" and the "static" aspects of his productions.

What is fatal to so large a number of these masterpieces is the manifest emptiness of the musical element, a fact which injures their prestige and jeopardises their future. The scores of *The Bavadere, The Daughter of Pharaoh* or *The Hunch-Backed Horse* are signed Minkus and Cesare Puni, both salaried composers who produced hundreds of acts to order. Though their simplified and accentuated rhythmical language corresponds at every point to the essentials of the dance, their musical imagination and their methods of orchestration exhibit an annoying and monotonous banality.

For this reason the intervention of Tchaikovsky was decisive. The composer of the *Symphonie pathétique* and *Eugéne Oneguine*, already on the road to fame, took a passionate interest in the problem. It was his ambition to apply the best of his musical imagination, all the delicacies of instrumentation and all his quaint and lyrical qualities to the composition of dance music, whose rhythm should faithfully adapt itself to the natural rhythm of the human body, moving according to the laws of classical gymnastics. He sacrificed his liberty as symphonic composer in order to follow the indications of the ballet master who asked him for a definite number of measures for each movement, and suggested the character of the accompaniment to him in every point. Thus he made an applied art out of dance music—at once the servant and the mistress of the ballet—but at the same time he gave a new direction to musical art which was one day to lead to Stravinsky; achieving for the Russian ballet what Léo Delibes had attempted in France, the rehabilitation of its musical standard.

Reforms of this nature in an institution like the Théatre Marie —in which tradition and even inertia, consecrated by a century of glory, suppressed all desire for change—needed the support of a firm and intelligent will. The man of destiny in this case was Alexander Ivanovitch Vsevolojskoi, who was appointed director of the Imperial Theatres when Alexander III. became Czar. This "honest man"—in the sense given to the phrase by the contemporaries of La Bruyére—was not merely the great Maecenas who gained all sympathies but also a kindly and enlightened dilletante, who did not neglect to search for documents and to handle the pencil on the occasion of each new production. He is responsible for thousands of sketches of historical costumes and personally supervised the scene painters, exhibiting the greatest competence in the process. In a word, he was a fervent lover of the ballet and an admirer of Petitpa. Once Peter Ilyitch Tchaikovsky had been won over to the cause, the hour for masterpieces had struck. The Prince Charming had arrived who was to awaken the Sleeping Princess.

A First Night at the Théatre Marie

It was Perrault's tale which provided the subject. One must not be surprised by the fact that this Russian work, so essentially national, should be of French inspiration! The gift of creative assimilation is one of the most evident characteristics of the Russian genius. Dostoievsky points out this faculty, which Pushkin had exemplified in the highest degree. Besides, Perrault's tales lived fresh in all memories. Ivan Turgenev, the "kindly giant," had translated the famous collection for Russian children as early as 1864.

Petitpa extracted from it a fairy ballet. Adult spectators and subscribers who remembered Taglioni and who had grown up under Nicholas I. were rather shocked. Yet the fairy tale is the last refuge of the departing gods, of lapsed mythologies, of gracious autocrats now dissolved in smoke, of vanished glories and faded dreams and elemental spirits relegated by triumphant scepticism to an inglorious obscurity. There is no longer room in the world for all this elsewhere than in the paradise of childhood. And what is this fanciful and puerile Sleeping Princess but the solar myth, the eternal allegory of the seasons disguised as a fairy-tale? What is the difference between Prince Charming waking Princess Aurora with a kiss, and Siegfried waking the Valkyrie sleeping on her rock? The one crosses the flower-bedecked gardens of the castle, while the other crosses the barrier of fire invoked by Loge. The gentle little prince with his lace cuffs is of the same divine essence as the grandiloquent young savage in his untanned bearskin.

It would be superfluous to retrace the acts and gestures of the characters of the ballet, as they are familiar to all. Its action is divided into five episodes; the baptism of Aurora and the gifts of the fairies; the fifteenth birthday of the Princess, when she pricks herself with a thorn and falls asleep; Prince Charming's hunting party, the apparition of Fairy Lilac and the shade of Aurora; the Prince's journey, with panorama and musical entr'acte; Aurora and her court awakened by the Prince; the betrothal and ball. This action, briefly summarised here, lends itself admirably to mass movements, regal entries and scenic variations, while openings for dances abound. As early as the prologue, we have an adagio of seven fairies. Nothing could be more harmonious than the *aeveloppés* of these seven principal dancers or their different variations culminating in the slow waltz of Fairy Lilac and followed immediately by the grotesque episode of the wicked fairy, Carabosse.

The second tableau opens with a celebrated ensemble, the *valse villageoise*. Garlands and baskets full of flowers in the hands of the dancers, rising and falling rhythmically at different heights, form a moving flower-garden, an ever-changing and animated scene. Then comes the principal action, the entry of Aurora, who tours the stage in a circular movement full of youthful ardour; accepts with a double pirouette a rose from each of the princes aspiring to her hand, turning on her toe, leaning to the right of each prince alternately and remaining balanced during the changing of hands; then waltzes with Carabosse's distaff, runs across the stage in terror and finally falls to the ground inanimate. Divine gambols, flowers of youth! Not a moment but is engraved ineradicably in the memory of those ballet-lovers who six times a month used to applaud an attitude, a gesture, a step, from the sky-blue stalls of the Théatre Marie, and are now scattered by so many storms throughout the world, at the mercy of ill winds.

These two tableaux are set in a "Henri IV." dreamland; the third carries us into a fanciful "Louis XIV." scene. A halt during a hunt: duchesses, countesses, baronesses, in a forest clearing, teasing, and playing blind-man's-buff with, the abbé preceptor; then dancing the grave and measured steps of yore, bowing and curtseying to Prince Charming, moving with a pretty clatter of the heels; and finally mingling with the joyous capers of the villagers in a mad concluding farandole. But the horns blow, the hunt is afoot once more. The kind fairy appears to the prince, who is devoured by amorous but aimless melancholy, and, to console him, evokes the shade of his beloved. Enter the white ballet-nymphs, dressed in the inverted corolla of tarlatan so dear to the sylphid Taglioni,—set in an 1830 moonlight scene in the very middle of the "Grand Siécle." Then flight and pursuit, the white followers of Aurora forming large and small circles or ranging themselves in columns, while arms outstretched and legs form quaint arabesque; her magic disappearance; the prince's journey in the fairy gondola; musical entr'acte with the languorous motif of the Fairy Lilac, and then a fresh picture, the awakening of the sleeping castle, and a somewhat rapid *pas d'action* in preparation for the magnificent scenes of the last act.

The whole of the fabulous and familiar world of Perrault assembled to greet and salute the shining white bride, the characters of his tales defiling in ceremony before the royal throne. The classical *pas de quatre* of the metals and precious stones opens the ball. This is followed by the little White Kitten, carried on a cushion, and Puss-in-Boots, while the music imitates the purring and mewing of their fond jealousy, as they strike each other with their paws, wheedle and brush against each other, hump their backs, leap lightly to and fro, playing their game of love with such delicate ferocity. Then come Red Riding Hood and Master Wolf—the dread meeting of the wicked simpleton and the frightened but sly child. Hop o' my Thumb and his brothers dance a merry step under the very nose of the Ogre. Cinderella, with the kitchen bellows in her hand, is recognised by the prince and presented with the golden slipper in a mazurka movement. And finally the Blue Bird and Princess Florine dance one of the three or four most beautiful classical *pas de deux* known in the whole work of Petitpa, indeed in the whole "literature" of classical dancing. The winged dancer collapsing, after his prodigious leaps, on to the stage in a mass of feathery down, with an almost imperceptible *plie,* or borne across it in a whirlwind of entrechats or lifting up the princess on his wings—here we have the true classical dance incarnate, with its thirst for the supernatural and with all its ethereal beauty. Then the adagio of newly-wed brides and bridegrooms comes as an excuse for the introduction of tuneful lines; and the general rush of the final sarabande, in which all the characters facing the audience, mingle the essential movements of their respective dances, brings the divertissement to a conclusion. On the general *coda,* that singular efflorescence of the *ballabile,* like a medley of the whole act, the curtain falls a last time.

The success in 1890 was enormous. Master of the ballet, dancers, painters and costumiers all came in for their share. The Milanese dancer, Brianza, answering like Grisi, not long since, to the sweet name of Carlotta, danced the part of Aurora and was enthusiastically applauded; the public noted with pleasure that the Italian virtuosity of Brianza—that "little brown imp"—was becoming more and more impregnated with the grand and nobler style of Saint-Petersburg. Paul Gerdt, illustrious dancer and mime, played the prince; Cecchetti, whom Paris saw in command thirty years later as master of the dolls in *Petrushka,* was disguised as Carabosse. Mesdemoiselles Johanson and Kulitchevska, who later achieved such fame, danced beside Kszessinsky as King Florestan, and Platon Karsavine as Prince Fortuné—the fathers of the two celebrated ballerinas bearing their respective names. And lastly, there was Marie Petitpa, whose somewhat luxuriant beauty and magic-wand haunted the dreams in those far distant days of the very small boy who has now become the author of these lines.

The *decors* (parks, buildings, esplanades, in the Renaissance and "Grand Siécle" manner) were the work of painters who, though since forgotten, possessed incontestable talent, namely Andreeff and Botchareff, of the Academy of Fine Arts, and Chichkoff, specialist in perspective, the painter of the "panorama" of the sleeping forest. The costumes by Vsevolojskoi, director and draughtsman, were inspired by Gustave Doré, and included many happy designs, like Red Riding Hood and the White Cat and Aurora's red tunic, whose colour has become traditional and was respected even by Bakst. In many cases, however, he sought inspiration from original sources, as for example the old prints of a tilting-contest, in which the King took part.

If anything was criticised it was the music. The oldest of the old school maintained that Tchaikovsky's "symphonic combinations" deprived the score of any resemblance to dance music, that the rhythm was not sufficiently marked. The young rebels, on the other hand, who very soon secured the upper hand, saluted Tchaikovsky's "heresies" as marking the liberation of music from the bondage of convention.

It is indeed curious in our day to look back on this revolution and quarrel while Igor Stravinsky loudly proclaims the genius of Tchaikovsky, upholding—in defiance of the shade of Wagner—the spontaneous melody of the Russian master against the *leitmotifs* of the mage of Bayreuth, his delicate instrumentation against the noisy orchestration of the German composers. Will the combative author of the *Sacré du Printemps* have the last word in this new debate round the name of Tchaikovsky? I cannot say.

But whatever may happen, the score of *The Sleeping Princess* will remain a remarkable example of musical art applied to the classical dance.

During the thirty years that followed that triumphal evening, the ballet has again and again changed its protagonists. There was Antonietta dell' Era; then, when once the Russian dancers had become mistresses in their own home, there were Préobrajenska, Anna Pavlova, Karsavina, Egorova and, above all, the extraordinary Mathilde Kszessinskaia, who, in the part of Aurora, was the very incarnation of happy and exuberant youth. A few years ago, when Vsevolojskoi's charming old costumes were falling to pieces, they were replaced by scenes and costumes designed by Korovine, of the Imperial Academy, a Muscovite painter, who crushed beneath the weight of cumbersome learning, crude colours and useless bric-à-brac, all that remained of the fragile and elegant dream conceived in the unique atmosphere of Saint-Petersburg, "that most" (in the words of Dostoievsky) "fantastic city in the world."

Then came the great revolutionary tempest, which swept away centuries of civilisation. Yet such is the force of a living tradition, that the debris of the illustrious Imperial Ballet survived, and one saw young dancers like Gerdt, Spessiva and Maklezova, dancing the part of Aurora before a turbulent audience thronged with Red Guards, and seeking protection against an icy temperature which froze the water in their dressing-room basins, by wearing thick knitted jackets with long sleeves beneath their filmy costumes of red gauze. All this heroic loyalty to the art of dancing, to its honour and to the ideal aspirations of the great "Petitpa style," represents so much ineffectual beauty in the midst of hideous, implacable reality. *The Sleeping Princess* sleeps in a dying land—a sleep from which there can be no awakening.

It was at this moment, when the destiny of the Russian ballet had seemingly run its course, that Diaghilev appeared, and called upon Bakst to bring Aurora back to life.

The Sleeping Princess

When staging *The Sleeping Princess* at the London Alhambra, Diaghilev pursued two aims. He reconstructed all that was imperishable in the work, that is to say, Petitpa's dances and Tchaikovsky's score; and completely renewed everything ephemeral, such as scenic effect and the co-ordination of the whole.

To restore the authentic steps of the ballet, he had recourse to the choregraphic annotations (recorded by the Stepanoff method) of M. Sergueïeff, former stage-manager of the Théatre Marie, and above all to the memory of the former interpreters. He completed his excellent company, which already embraced such stars as Idzikovsky and Lopokova, by recruiting the *élite* of the Imperial ballet —or those who had escaped from the Bolsheviks—including the three Auroras, Olga Spessiva, Liubov Egorova, Vera Trefilova, and the dancers Peter Vladimiroff and Anatole Vilzac. The part of the wicked fairy Carabosse was filled by Carlotta Brianza, the Aurora of 1890—a happy thought, symbolic of the traditions which were to be revived. The music was enriched by several previously unknown fragments that had been suppressed in the score owing to a whim of Alexander III.: in addition to which he made use of another work, the result of a collaboration between Tchaikovsky, Petitpa and Leon Ivanoff, called *The Nutcracker,* after Hoffmann (1892), from which he extracted the variation for the *celesta* (known in England as the dance of the Sugar-Plum Fairy) and the Chinese and Arab dances of the divertissement. The hunting dances and games were entrusted to Mlle. Bronislave Nijinska, who treated them broadly in the manner of the "Grand Siécle." Tchaikovsky, when dealing with rhythms of the old dances of the French court had avoided a direct pastiche, had, in short, evoked without imitating. With a part of the *coda*, neglected by Petitpa and of truly Russian inspiration, Nijinska constructed a really fine scene of choregraphic buffoonery. The famous classical steps to which I previously alluded were all respected, except in the case of the groupings and movements of the *corps de ballet* "supporting" the leading characters. The ordering of the action was naturally subject to the decorative inspiration of Bakst, who was the deciding factor in its success. What Bakst, moved by so many memories, stimulated by so many difficulties, conceived and executed, is indeed a fine achievement which will take due place among the annals of theatrical art.

The Contribution of Léon Bakst

In less than six weeks—his time was necessarily restricted—Léon Bakst composed, or, rather, improvised the six scenes and the three hundred costumes (a whole world of pictorial fiction) which the ballet contains. A less bold, more timorous worker, seeking the exact historical document, nosing about in portfolios, compiling dossiers, would have succumbed to the difficulties. Bakst, above all else an imaginative artist, triumphed. Instead of building up an imitation, he created a dream of reality. Not, in truth, that reality in which the good Perrault lived his *bourgeois* life: for Russian tradition juxtaposed the "Musketeer" period in the first two tableaux with the Grand Siécle style of the remainder, whereas Bakst, ignoring "the historical sense" preferred to establish the whole action in a single frame. And so he plunged all the constituents of the presentation into one vast enchantment, an Eighteenth-Century dreamland, the true domain of the Marquis de Carabas.

This effect is traceable to three things, a buoyant, grandiose organisation of space, an expert orchestration of colours and an inexhaustible wealth of decorative invention.

Bakst's sketches prove it; but in order to appreciate their latent scenic significance and to realise how, while exhibiting from the very beginning of the prologue an unprecedented display of ocular devices, it not only maintains this standard until the end but actually proceeds in *crescendo*, it is necessary to recall and analyse the impressions of a performance. Instead, therefore, of telling the story of the ballet, which is familiar to everyone, let us try briefly to reconstruct the visual ensemble, act by act.

The scenery of the prologue, which is architectural, creates something of a surprise. One expected of course to see a Versailles, some tedious royal château—the inevitable achievement of chicken-hearted orthodoxy. Nothing of the kind. The architecture, the conception of which dominates two other acts, recalls Tiepolo or Piranese rather than Mansart. It consists of a spacious hall, with ingeniously grouped marble colonnades, crowned by balustrades, and is established on advancing planes. At the back it is terminated, like a landing, by an invisible staircase stretching the whole width of the stage. The characters entering are supposed to come up these stairs; first the plumes and head-dress appear, then the powdered wig, then the lord or lady complete. Beyond this great gulf another monumental staircase arises majestically, parallel to the footlights. A multitude of Swiss Guards "in effigy," wearing their scarlet costume, adorns its steps. At once pretentious and diminutive, they complete the impression of grandeur, of giddy heights, produced by the masterly utilisation of a very limited space. One is recalled to the subject of the first tableau, the baptism of Princess Aurora. The stage, empty when the curtain rises, slowly fills to the sounds of a march. First come the Queen's ladies-in-waiting, with powdered wigs and shortened paniers like those of the little figures which the Boquets drew for the entertainments of Louis le Bien-Aimé; indeed, they are in the style rather of operatic dancers of the Eighteenth Century than of the great dames of the Seventeenth. But what matter? They date from a period which is almost legendary.

The general tone is red heightened by green. Lords with their long wigs, plumed hats and green—almost black—coats, line up for the passage of King Florestan and the Queen, dressed in white and gold and ermine-lined blue velvet cloaks with long trains carried by blue pages. Enter the fairies, wearing the airy uniform of the ballerina, invariable in all climes and all periods of fiction, their white *tutus* adorned by charming emblems of magic power and picked out with bunches of cherries or tufts of feathers. Pages, also in white, carry their insignia. Every kaleidoscopic evolution is carried out to the rhythm of the action, until the final moment when the crowd of gaily-bedizened courtiers, bowing before the fairy-guarded cradle, seem to surge towards it in one scarlet wave while a luxuriant group of Moors in black and gold, standing motionless in the midst of this flux of colour, serves as striking contrast: a medley of brilliant tones which complement the regal spaciousness of the décor.

Second tableau. A fête champêtre, the birthday of Aurora. A light colonnade with balustrades curves gracefully through the groves, and a white palace stands in the background; we have here the same play of verticles and curves. The trimmed groves are indeed those of Versailles; but they are grown *upwards,* overhanging each other. Heavy masses of compact verdure, tunnelled by arched passages, alternating, as in some Italian parks, with the slim cones of the cypress trees, scale the blue-grey sky, the sweet sky of France.

A circle of peasants and peasant women in peony red and green fills the stage. The famous waltz begins. The court arrives—the Princes aspiring to Aurora's hand, the splendid Velasquez Spaniard with his short brown cape, the red Hindoo. And red, too, is Aurora's tunic lightly draped *en panier* and embroidered in royal gold like that of the Fairy Lilac, who wears the colour of her emblematic flower. Everything here is designed to set off the person of Aurora, who is crowned with a singularly beautiful perruque of pale gold.

After the spell of Carabosse is cast, the enchantment of the Fairy Lilac operates in its turn, and a double chain of bushes, covered with purple clusters, rises from out of the earth and hides the scene.

A hundred years pass. Prince Charming's hunting party. A clearing in the forest on the edge of a lake. It is autumn, and the scenery suggests a profound and sombre melancholy, whereby the tormented Prince, enamoured of a dream, is further distracted. Bare tree trunks, brown shadows, water of a leaden blue.

The coquetries of the arch ladies of the hunt seem to fill the stage like the whirl of dead leaves in the wind; amazons in gold, chestnut or olive brocade, mingling with the bolder green of the huntsmen. Suddenly there appears shooting forth amid this riot of autumn leaves, like a flame of cadmium, the yellow costume of the countess with her three-cornered hat and black scarf—quaint and appealing as a figure from Pietro Longhi which has strayed into a picture by Berain, "draughtsman to the King."

Later, in the apparition scene, a white swarm of *tutus* invades the stage, their powdery whiteness sprinkled with little nosegays; and one calls to mind the lithograph of Carlotta Grisi dancing *Gisella*.

At last the Prince embarks for the enchanted castle. Here, instead of the panorama, impracticable on the stage of the Alhambra, there is a simple change of scenery. Against the noble sadness of a pearly-grey sky, a white donjon stands out, massive but elegant, with battlements, towers and belfreys. In the foreground a light green forest; further back, sombre blue-green trees, bristling, menacing, form a sinister palissade around the accursed castle. It is a finely simple and poetical expression of the desolate.

Musical interlude. The journey through the thorny bushes and thickets, the arrival at the palace and the kiss that frees. It is a very short scene. The Princess is sleeping on a daïs under a gigantic *ciel de lit*. Betrothal, dénouement. The action is over; and it remains for the Dance, the divine Dance, to put the final splashes on the canvas. A festival is called for, such as has never been seen before, and so we come to the last, the supreme tableau.

The scene is an empty hall, open to the sky. In inspiration it bears a modified resemblance to the first act. The back of the stage is rounded off in a half circle of white and gold, veined with grey. It is almost a forest of lightly turned columns, but with nothing "baroque" about it, nothing of the heaviness of the "official style" of the period. It is more like an old vision, such as some late Venetian might have conceived for a "Triumph of Alexander." Precious materials, solid and polished, wide generous lines, liberal spaces. It is one of Bakst's finest successes in theatrical architecture, comparable to the pathetic twisted columns of the "False Gods" act in *Saint Sebastien,* or the black and gold portico, with its sheaves of small columns, that frames the febrile action of *Pisanella*.

Diaghilev cut out the cortége of the fairy-tales given in Petitpa's version, being afraid to spoil the effect of the *entrées* which constitute the divertissement. As this defile took place to the strains of a "polonaise," Polish nobles, helmeted and spurred, with flying green capes, reminiscent of the winged dragons dear to Stefano della Bella, now open the ball with white-mantled partners. The royal couple, adorned with full heraldic paraphernalia and wearing long emerald green cloaks, take their thrones in stately grandeur: the King with plumed and vizored helmet, armoured from head to foot and bearing his insignia of royalty, the Queen bending beneath the weight of a perruque with colossal feathers. Before them is unrolled the skein of dance episodes, short sparkling visions. A classical *pas de quatre,* boldly filched by invaders from the Comedia dell' Arte—a mere suggestion of streaked colour on a white background—gives place to the amorous dialogue of the little White Kitten and Puss-in-Boots, belted with the red cordon of a royal order, to Red Riding Hood fleeing from the Wolf in full court dress, to Princess Florine and the Blue Bird, a symphony in blue-major, to Bluebeard with his wives, dressed and coiffed like ladies in "the days of old," one of whose family executions is stayed by the arrival of two comic cavaliers on cardboard chargers (grotesque scene of the kind Bakst loves), while Ivan the Innocent and his brothers, gyrating like the devil, set the skirts of their embroidered caftans all a-flying.

And so these rapid sketches continue. Our curiosity is progressively sharpened by their diversity, we are almost exasperated by the range of the artist's exuberant, ironical invention. The lacquer-faced Chinaman with his gold, pagoda-like head-dress, and the two Chinese women like daubed porcelain figures rigged out in French paniers and little cone-shaped hats, plying their fans to the merry tinkling of bells, are a marvel of bantering, conventional exoticism. It can only be eclipsed by the Turkish scene—Scheherazade arriving in a Louis XIV. sedan-chair, decorated with arabesques in the purest Persian style, wearing a turban with aigrette and white silk trousers beneath her court dress—the ideal sultana of the "Bourgeois Gentilhomme."

But how can justice be done to so vast an imaginative fabric, that displays devotion no less to detail and suggestion than to general effect, by a mere enumeration of odd corners remembered? May this brief sketch at least serve to recall the outline of a truly remarkable fantasy.

I have expressed my emotion as happy spectator at the sight of so much well-directed enthusiasm serving a great cause in its hour of need—the traditional Russian ballet, the so-called "classical" ballet. It only remains for me to condense in a few lines the contribution of Bakst, the balance-sheet of this great enterprise and the lesson it teaches.

Not only did Bakst powerfully reinforce the tradition of the dance, but he resolutely revived another tradition, that of archi*tectural scenery, an incomparable setting for the actor, for the human body.* He returned boldly to harmoniously organised masses, to surprising foreshortenings, to the magic play of superimposed planes and suggestive curves, to the splendid austerity of line perspective. We find him—after a century of sham realism—resuscitating the work of great decorative architects, masters of stage vision, like Gonzaga, Valeriani or Gradizzi in Russia, and Bibbiena or Serlio in Italy.

Who can say whether this is but a passing episode, the whim of a spirited imagination or the birth of a new school of scenic painting? At least it is a living idea, which will leave its mark.

One further point. The imagination, transcending history and fiction, stands out free from all pedantry and erudition, from all servile imitation revelling in its own plagiarism. Bakst, here as elsewhere, is the creator of an atmosphere, not a gravedigger rummaging among tombs.

But to my mind, Bakst's greatest claim to theatrical glory lies in his feeling for synthesis, in his impeccable instinct for harmony, which blends the innumerable elements of the performance into one single, coherent whole. Therein lies the supreme virtue of *The Sleeping Princess*.

ANDRÉ LEVINSON.

LIST OF ILLUSTRATIONS

BASKET OF FLOWERS (Title Page)
1. PORPHYROPHORES
2. MARCHIONESS (Hunting)
3. BLUE-BEARD
4. MINISTER
5. PAGE BOY OF THE FAIRY CANARY
6. PUSS-IN-BOOTS
7. SCENERY FOR THE BAPTISM
8. THE KING'S GUARD
9. PAGE-BOY OF THE FAIRY CHERRY
10. THE QUEEN'S GUARD
11. COLUMBINE
12. HARLEQUIN
13. SCENERY FOR THE ROYAL GARDEN
14. THE PRINCESS AURORA
15. CHINAMAN
16. CHINESE LADY
17. PAGE BOY OF THE FAIRY LARCH
18. THE FAIRY MOUNTAIN-ASH
19. BARONESS (Hunting)
20. PAGE-BOY OF THE FAIRY LILAC
21. THE FAIRY CARNATION
22. THE WOLF
23. THE QUEEN AND HER PAGES
24. THE RUSSIAN BUFFOON
25. SCENERY FOR THE BLOOMING OF THE LILAC
26. THE NEIGHBOURING PRINCE
27. MARSHAL CANTALABUTTE
28. COUNTS (Hunting)
29. PRINCE CHARMING AT COURT

FAIRY CARABOSSE (Contents Page)
30. PRINCE AURORA IN BRIDAL DRESS
31. THE CASTLE IN WHICH THE PRINCESS SLEEPS
32. PAGE-BOY OF THE FAIRY MOUNTAIN-ASH
33. MAZURKA (Ladies)
34. MAZURKA (Gentlemen)
35. THE KING WITH HIS PAGES
36. SCENERY FOR THE BETROTHAL
37. PAGES OF THE PRINCESS
38. MIRLITONS
39. SCHEHERAZADE
40. GALISSON, THE PRINCE'S TUTOR
41. PAGE-BOY OF THE FAIRY HUMMING-BIRD
42. SEDAN-CHAIR OF SCHEHERAZADE
43. HUNTSMAN
44. THE FLEMISH BRIDEGROOM
45. THE INDIAN BRIDEGROOM
46. THE ENGLISH BRIDEGROOM
47. THE MASTER OF CEREMONIES
48. PAGE-BOY OF THE WICKED FAIRY CARABOSSE
49. THE PRINCE'S NEGROES
50. THE KING IN THE GARDEN
51. PRINCE CHARMING (Hunting)
52. THE FAIRY CHERRY
53. COURTIERS (Baptism)
54. MARSHAL CANTALABUTTE (after the departure of the wicked fairy Carabosse)

At the Pelican Press.

PLATE 1

PORPHYROPHORES

PLATE 11

MARCHIONESS (Hunting)

PLATE III

BLUE-BEARD

PLATE IV

MINISTER

PLATE V

PAGE-BOY OF THE FAIRY CANARY

PLATE VI

PUSS-IN-BOOTS

PLATE VII

SCENERY FOR THE BAPTISM

PLATE VIII

THE KING'S GUARD

PLATE IX

PAGE-BOY OF THE FAIRY CHERRY

PLATE X

THE QUEEN'S GUARD

PLATE XI

COLUMBINE

PLATE XII

HARLEQUIN

PLATE XIII

SCENERY FOR THE ROYAL GARDEN

PLATE XIV

THE PRINCESS AURORA

PLATE XV

CHINAMAN

PLATE XVI

CHINESE LADY

PLATE XVII

PAGE-BOY OF THE FAIRY LARCH

PLATE XVIII

THE FAIRY MOUNTAIN-ASH

PLATE XIX

BARONESS (Hunting)

PLATE XX

PAGE-BOY OF THE FAIRY LILAC

PLATE XXI

THE FAIRY CARNATION

PLATE XXII

THE WOLF

PLATE XXIII

THE QUEEN AND HER PAGES

PLATE XXIV

THE RUSSIAN BUFFOON

PLATE XXV

THE SCENE FOR THE BLOOMING OF THE LILAC

PLATE XXVI

THE NEIGHBOURING PRINCE

PLATE XXVII

MARSHALL CANTALABUTTE

PLATE XXVIII

COUNTS (Hunting)

PLATE XX1X

PRINCE CHARMING AT COURT

PLATE XXX

PRINCESS AURORA IN BRIDAL DRESS

PLATE XXXI

THE CASTLE IN WHICH THE PRINCESS SLEEPS

PLATE XXXII

PAGE-BOY OF THE FAIRY MOUNTAIN-ASH

PLATE XXXIII

MAZURKA (Ladies)

PLATE XXXIV

MAZURKA (Gentlemen)

PLATE XXXV

THE KING WITH HIS PAGES

PLATE XXXVI

SCENERY FOR THE BETROTHAL

PLATE XXXVII

PAGES OF THE PRINCESS

PLATE XXXVIII

MIRLITONS

PLATE XXXIX

SCHEHERAZADE

PLATE XL

GALISSON, THE PRINCE'S TUTOR

PLATE XLI

PAGE-BOY OF THE FAIRY HUMMING-BIRD

PLATE XLII

SEDAN-CHAIR OF SCHEHERAZADE

PLATE XLIII

HUNTSMAN

PLATE XLIV

THE FLEMISH BRIDEGROOM

PLATE XLV

THE INDIAN BRIDEGROOM

PLATE XLVI

THE ENGLISH BRIDEROOM

PLATE XLVII

THE MASTER OF CEREMONIES

PLATE XLVIII

PAGE-BOY OF THE WICKED FAIRY CARABOSSE

PLATE XLIX

THE PRINCE'S NEGROES

PLATE L

THE KING IN THE GARDEN

PLATE LI

PRINCE CHARMING (Hunting)

PLATE LII

THE FAIRY CHERRY

PLATE LIII

COURTIERS (Baptism)

PLATE LIV

MARSHALL CANTALABUTTE
(After the departure of the Wicked Fairy Carabosse)

www.ingramcontent.com/pod-product-compliance
Lightning Source LLC
Chambersburg PA
CBHW042315280426
43661CB00102B/1287